CW01151159

LEADERSHIP LESSONS

LEADERSHIP LESSONS

Strategies for Inspiring Others

B. VINCENT

QuillQuest Publishers

CONTENTS

1 Introduction 1
2 Building Trust and Credibility 4
3 Motivating and Empowering Individuals 9
4 Creating a Positive and Inclusive Culture 15

Copyright © 2024 by B. Vincent

All rights reserved. No part of this book may be reproduced in any manner whatsoever without written permission except in the case of brief quotations embodied in critical articles and reviews.

First Printing, 2024

CHAPTER 1

Introduction

Leaders have the power to guide, inspire, and influence others. Leadership is based on the principles of empowering and inspiring others to achieve their full potential. Leading healthcare organizations have embraced the need to invest in their leaders. Through self-awareness, building relationships, aligning system goals, adapting strategies to meet the individual needs of staff and nursing unity, nurses can develop the astuteness necessary to be leaders in the nursing profession and can inspire others to reach their full potential. Leadership attributes must be modeled by everyone that demonstrates the profession of nursing. Educating and developing the nursing staff is important to retain our future nurse leaders in an era of shortage. The nursing profession must form partnerships and alliances on a global level to ensure that resources are in place to realize a bright future for the nursing profession.

The healthcare field requires strong leadership, innovative ideas, and the foresight to guide and direct the healthcare industry through national and global challenges. The essence of nursing leadership helps to shape the nursing profession and to inspire others to reach their potential. Leadership is not confined to management;

leadership extends throughout the profession and anyone has the ability to mold and shape the profession in a leadership role. Nurses in all aspects of practice, regardless of title or climb of administrative leadership, have the potential to be great leaders. To be a leader, one does not have to be a manager or have people working under them. Anyone can be a leader. Being a leader does not have to do with title; being a leader has to do with how you interact with your peers, motivate them to do better, listen to them, and value their ideas and points of view.

1.1 The Importance of Leadership

Leaders who have faith in the potentialities in their unit are also prepared to work at turning these prospective motivators into loyal and driven comrades. Through encouraging voice, leaders can demonstrate that an attachment develops between themselves and their follower. Then realizing that for anyone to want to be a follower is a consciously selected identity. It can be effortlessly distorted, with possibly critical side-effects. This also implies that a follower is not an object or a problem that can be ripped apart and nurtured; it is not something that is individual from the self. It is not something that comes only after an individual is "set loose" and ready for interaction. Anything that can express itself through a discourse or an initiative of obedience has to do with voice and moral freedom. The effort of endeavor, voice, and freedom is that they involve consistent participation. Conscious bodies cannot interact with a thing. A person shapes his or her followership with intelligence and purpose.

The effectiveness of leadership training and education is one of the most tangible ways of directly promoting strong, spirited growth. Good leadership is vital in every team and organization. It is a privilege that comes with an extraordinary set of obligations. When leaders honestly embrace the responsibility of their positions and seldom predict the results of expecting followership, they are now prepared to carry out the actions that are fundamental to success. Since "leadership influences individuals toward the achievement of a goal," just as each individual needs to decide to be motivated, leaders need to comprehend that the prospective motivators have different drivers that can inspire or kill motivation.

1.2 Overview of Inspiring Others

When you wake up in the morning and listen to the song of the birds and see the sunrise, it is as though nature is inviting you to a new beginning, a new story, a new chapter, a new page. It is an awakening, a rebirth, a welcoming to new possibilities or positive transformation. Great leaders help others see a better version of themselves and spark an enthusiasm around it. It could range from overcoming an obstacle, solving a technical puzzle, achieving one's targets, or making the impossible possible. This process needs to be subtle and inspiring, not controlling and forced. You win by having these flap their wings, not flapping your arms for them. Leaders who can inspire, guide, and motivate the team to achieve beyond their customary performances are very few. Inspiring others establishes a culture of enthusiasm and success. It is very important for people to look forward to their discussions with their leaders.

One of the greatest responsibilities of a leader is to inspire others to break boundaries, achieve more, and create greater value. A leader gives people a reason to get up in the morning and contribute. Thus, one of the greatest skills a person can have is to be an inspirational leader and to motivate others to perform at their peak. It is an art and a practice to express an interest in people, enable them to feel better about themselves, and bring out the best in them. Optimization comes from all the parts of the whole being optimized. Therefore, by optimal interactions with the team, the greater function (the team) gets optimized.

CHAPTER 2

Building Trust and Credibility

Ethics in leadership practice are key for a successful business. The real challenge of becoming a trusted leader lies deep within the psyche of each person and propels that person's daily behavior and actions. In other words, if you fear for your safety psychologically and socially and believe that those around you are motivated by self-interest, you will unwittingly engage in the behaviors that grind trust out of the organization. While this fear may have been well placed at one time, it is important that all employees feel that the organization is stable and that they will not be punished for exhibiting loyalty or moral judgment. True leaders are ethical leaders, striding beyond what is conventional, what is expected, or what is typical. These individuals share common traits, among which are respecting all individuals, upholding cultural sensitivity, and maintaining a moral compass. With leadership that teaches justice, equality, and the fight for a positive, shared vision, followers are engaged and feel welcome in any organization.

Without trust in leadership, as well as in one's coworkers, an organization cannot hope to be effective. As an internationally recognized authority in the field of trust and trustworthiness, Dr. Laura R. Palk provides a handful of tangible things that a company can do to begin to shape a more trusting and trustworthy culture and thus more effective, inspired employees. Defined as shared internal beliefs and expectations for what a given organization values, trust can be built only with time and positive experiences. As a CEO, there are things that you can start doing today, for instance, apologizing when you make a mistake or admitting a mistake when something goes wrong. These little things can be major steps toward an organization with employees that feel they can comfortably express themselves and be an active participant in growing the organization.

2.1 Establishing Authenticity

Why would someone want to be a leader? Today's world is moving towards a flatter hierarchy, where leadership roles are shared and even negotiated, but the emergence of these struggles is nothing more than the confirmation of the current leadership crisis and the lack of viable responses to turn it around. Assuming a leadership position is nothing more than a strong statement of love, I insist. Wanting the human being to give the best of himself/herself and of themselves, working with excitement and dedicating it to a project together, be it a minimal or a gigantic one like a corporation. Otherwise, creating an alignment of vision in all, including making everyone walk side by side in search of a common objective, does not yield results. This is also only achievable through love.

Managers must look after and cultivate all aspects of an employee-production-company. It is important to take care of the team's values, vision, quality and quantity of production, and why not, to look after their health. Even an air of a manager you generate intense effects on all employees. An enthusiastic and charming manager can change the entire face of the company. One who appears overpowered and with a devastating air, also modifies the ecosystem, causing the production to fall, the composition and vision of the employees, the company's reputation, and the evaluations of your customers.

If you don't believe in what you say, if your actions are not consistent with what you think - your leadership will not get far. My advice, if you are aspiring to lead, is "with love or without anger." That is why honesty is crucial, and you must be consistent every day. How can a manager lead the organization if he/she has trust issues with his team, if there is no team? Thus, honesty is provided by creating a relationship of trust between the leader and the members of the company. This is significant to create an ecosystem where the team is a support pillar that allows the manager to take risks and make better decisions.

2.2 Demonstrating Competence

Do not underestimate the emblematic power of technical expertise, or its power as a motivational force. Even though you cannot be expected to know more about a topic or a task than the people whom you lead, if you maintain and share your conceit, engage in the higher level discussions, and understand the context of the work being performed, the members of your team will look to you as a leader. You can show them that their leader is in fact a member of their community, and not just a democracy visitor, someone who earns their respect. A competent leader values the professional development and the skills growth of the team members, and that willingness to enable this growth can be a very potent tool when leading professional colleagues.

Being technically proficient is necessary for you to be an effective leader. Technical competency is important because it provides you with a foundation on which people can build their confidence in you. People evaluate your professional development, your commitment to the organization, and your value to the organization based upon this capability. Competence in the field you have selected also helps you to make decisions with confidence and to assist others who are seeking guidance. The people who work with you need this assurance and will know how to best work with you. For most professional groups, it is the primary method they have to evaluate you. After all, the bottom line for a professional leader is successful project implementation and the constituents expect you to maintain technical proficiency.

The following strategies will support you in demonstrating competence as a leader:

2.3 Communicating Openly and Transparently

Twenty-four business leaders are selected to participate in each Simulation event. The events can alternate between being internal or they can be a custom-selected group for exceptional customer leadership training. The participants can also range from any level in the organization, starting with junior managers upward to the most senior executives, including the CEO. The Simulations represent their personal Development Team. The Simulation event objectives include senior executives from the company and role model customers. This equips participants with forensic review and deep knowledge transfer about the corporate culture, opportunities, examples of recognized successes, accelerating results, leadership strengths drive successes, and, of course, the lessons learned.

There are a number of ways that the understanding of what is expected can be communicated. One technique is the Simulation event, which provides a methodology to set the pace for the development of leadership attributes. The Simulation sets the cadence of a company's leadership process, which can occur 3-4 times per year. Each Simulation is scheduled for a 2-day process with a specific Leadership topic setting the stage for it.

Communicating openly and transparently can naturally lead to the forging of good relationships. It is important that individuals know where they stand when expectations are not met, when positive results are achieved, and also when correctable actions are required. It has been said that by properly aligning the expectations of employees and then helping team members succeed in meeting those expectations, it enhances their professional growth and provides the potential reward of recognition, acknowledgement, and impact.

CHAPTER 3

Motivating and Empowering Individuals

It must be different from other types of individuals in specific ways. It must represent the idealized behavior of the leader, must be highly consistent, and must be behaviorally strong. If any of these three fundamental characteristics are absent, inspirational communication does not emerge. Also, a high level of arousal or high motivational state on the part of the follower is present in response to the leader's behavior. Inspiring communication need not be a part of a long communication attempt to concentrate on the leader for the duration; a positive emotional response to the communication process goes a long way to achieve high motivation on the part of the followers. However, of all sources of arousal, it is perhaps the emotional response to the communication process or leadership behavior that is created by the charismatic leader. The results suggest that leaders can use two general strategies to influence followers. First, when hiring new men to work, the group will change their negatives, basically displaying a higher level of consistency, rather than a higher level of both behavior and consistency.

Individuals are willing to go to extraordinary lengths of belief in their leader. For example, reports have shown that excellent morale during dangerous missions results in a higher degree of accuracy in combat. The leader inspires his followers, as in this case, only after thoroughly discussing and clarifying the mission and wants an inclusive decision on how it should be carried out. To set the example himself, the leader eats first, and then the second in command eats second to show that the leader cares for his team. Whether the leader is engaging in direct operations, giving a briefing or having a conversation with his followers, or sharing personal experiences, these are highly effective signals to the men in the organization. Effective inspirational communication typically produces some type of identification or connection between the leader and the follower.

3.1 Understanding Individual Needs

The simple answer is that people are different. They have needs and values that are based on beliefs, philosophies, and points of view. Not only does this make us unique, beneficial, and creative, it also makes us stubborn, flawed, angry, and capricious. One of the complex aspects of leadership is to respect the differences of other persons and to consider their point of view. A truism is that people perform better when their managers understand and support their performance goals. People need to feel that their work is meaningful. If they can understand a personal relevance or significance, then they are more likely to perform the work. Another truism is that a person's beliefs significantly affect the motivation behind any action. Our values engage us in the pursuit of what we believe. We need to feel a clear and honest connection to our actions. This is why vision alignment sessions are such an important step at the outset of a partnership with others. It is necessary to understand a person's talents and passions. Accomplishments are far greater if the project is in an area of natural talent. This operates as a key to success. This strengthens the goal development process.

Can inspiring others really be a question of understanding what people want? It is a simple question that deserves an honest answer. The risk is that leaders can underestimate what everyone is feeling. True leadership must begin by asking questions, by truly understanding what their followers desire and what they deserve. Could someone see the importance of what is being done? If someone feels that the work being done is important, then their ability to find motivation.

3.2 Providing Meaningful Feedback

Feedback will definitely be increased when listening. Have one-on-one meetings with employees, create opportunities for employees to give management feedback on their own performance and that of the organization. When listening to suggestions from many minds, more creative and cooperative decisions are made. Give time for employees to give feedback that can add value to the business. When a business is administered with a focus on feedback from everyone involved with the company, then the organization will move together. Administration is about effective communication. Feedback contributes to effective communication. Early startup organizations, in particular, rely heavily on honest assessments between the manager and the employees. This effective communication is built through feedback between each other. The sooner the crude problem is fixed by feedback from employees or vice versa, the sooner the survival of the organization and the more test of confidence and responsible employees.

When conducting a performance review with an employee, never overwhelm them with too much negative feedback at once. Limit feedback to only one negative and one positive thing at a time. After giving them the critique, always present the employee with an action plan for improvement. If an employee is critiqued through open-ended feedback or is presented with overwhelming constructive criticism, these employees tend to give up on their tasks. After we reinforce them with constructive criticism, we must also show them the road to improvement. Employees are people too. They want to feel valued and appreciated at the end of a work week or after a significant project. Your employees will not always ask when a positive performance will be recognized, so you must observe their work and verbalize your appreciation for the accomplishment. Celebrate the triumphs. It can be as simple as taking them to lunch, naming them as the employee of the month, or offering them a cash incentive. Do something to recognize their hard work and dedication to their job. Finally, remember that it is important to make sure that all of the accolades are publicly available to others within the organization.

3.3 Encouraging Innovation and Creativity

You must also encourage creativity and innovation. To use the most appropriate mediums for your message, you must be a master of communication thinking. Reshape and rechannel ideas through effective access to people and media that communicate your most creative thoughts. The process of communication to best influence an audience or followers incorporates a basic understanding of the same elements that are involved in the creative process: technological skills, time development, grasping of the overt and covert issues, unsure solutions and new developments, flexibility, feedback, research, realistic expectations and the need for vision to provide a well-defined focus of the goal.

Have a sense of urgency to get things done and provide inspiration and belief to all who work with you. You do this by constantly looking for new ways to communicate your vision. They encourage input and involvement from others and then give that vision direction. Then, sometimes by painful trial-and-error, you encourage new methods and techniques, learn to be innovative and flexible and keep the process focused on the big picture. In this way, you set the pace. Momentum in the creative process is desired, but innovation and creativity alone are not enough. These qualities must have direction and timing to be useful. They're the elements of achievement and must have goals or they lack value. Balance these factors to maintain your sense of timing and build a consistent record of achievements.

3.4 Delegating Responsibilities

Remember the days when you were smarter than a first grader? Not anymore. Even as your children are learning programming from before abandoning it for a music app, your first-line managers will almost always be better communicators, employees, and handlers than you could ever be. Consequently, any changes you make that affect your employees - any changes in procedures, rules, or even equipment - are likely to be met with resistance. You can treat these first-line managers in the same way you used to treat your direct reports, relying upon them to convey your sentiments and value to direct reports. Unfortunately for them, there is no one advocating about their hidden status. Information getting to the first-line managers is unlikely to be 100% accurate, with accuracy declining some the closer it gets to the floor. Even when first-line managers are given accurate information, the employees often see through it and instead assume that the manager is either misinformed or is just disregarding faults.

Leaders rarely learn to delegate by the time they are earning managerial hats. They will wear several hats, each new level of hot hat on the assembly line. The completed garments must act according to regulations, fixing payroll mixups, permissions to cross-train, or to use a shared resource. You now must also negotiate. The tasks nearly always involve resources. The group most affected by your new bureaucratic obligations is not your employees - it's your first-line managers. In addition to the extra time you will now spend in meetings, your new job description usually includes supervising.

CHAPTER 4

Creating a Positive and Inclusive Culture

I don't want to hear anymore about how there are not enough women to pick from. When I hear that, it just says to me, "I don't want to debias my recruitment process," or more subtly, "I am partial to male candidates." For every job, typically, you put a panel together to evaluate the candidates' knowledge, skills, and abilities. That same panel needs to evaluate the demonstration of potential, of learning agility, and decide on several things – not the least of which is that they are speaking the truth. And certainly investing in that is actually vital. Hence, the panel has to live by the same ethos. Better yet, forget about the panel altogether and let the incumbent make the hire. And "underrepresented members of the firm?" Why do we still hold a debate over this?

It's up to the leader to create an environment where anyone can succeed. This is, in our view, one of the key responsibilities of leadership – creating an environment where everyone feels welcome, valued, included, and able to succeed. This sounds to me like common sense, but clearly it is not yet in so many companies – so often, I hear the contrary. And quite honestly, I'm tired of wishing we were beyond some traditional mindsets about our roles and the obstacles to inclusion and equity for everyone to be able to thrive.

4.1 Fostering Collaboration and Teamwork

Leaders may then perceive the rise of in-group/out-group competition and interpret it as a reality of human behavior that organizations have to harness or manipulate to remain viable. It should not surprise us that sports, at its best, can be a model of the behaviors that result in business success, including inspired teamwork, uncompromising awareness of situational context and joint mentoring. Most organizations do not have the same physiological benefits from exercise, but the same principles apply. In sum, all organizations should strive to create healthy in-group/out-group dynamics that encourage teamwork and between-group communication. These intergroup attitudes are fundamentally splintered within participant minds. These attitudes can be partially reconciled by creating a context in which team member diversity is appreciated and evaluated. Intergroup communication is not easy and requires support and structure.

This program is designed to help you learn to develop and execute the behaviors that will distinguish you as an admired leader who can help the group navigate the uncertainties and difficulties they are facing. In turn, even those who are struggling can find relief and a sense of confidence. You will learn how to help the group develop a new perspective on the situation and align their response. Leading in times of change and uncertainty presents some of the greatest opportunities to display leadership and provide lasting benefits, both to the organization and to the group of people you lead. However, it can be tempting - especially in tough economic times - to put the focus on the effects of loss and how to manage them. When times are uncertain, people naturally turn it into an in-group/out-group rivalry. They are more willing to make financial or other sacrifices and more likely to follow your policies for the well-being of the group.

4.2 Promoting Diversity and Inclusion

Being a leader, it is our responsibility to set the example of openness to others and of appreciation of differences. As Thomas Bilyeu, Founder of Quest Nutrition, explained in one of his interviews, the main role for leaders is to show that it is okay for people to make mistakes, as nobody is perfect. It is okay to say "I don't know" and it is normal to change our opinions. Sometimes, it is due to our own fears or insecurity that we are not open to others or to diversity. Paco León stated that "fear is just a consequence of a lack of self-knowledge". The more we know each other, the less afraid we will be. A negative environment and a critical attitude can also prevent others from fully expressing their potential. Mihaly Csikszentmihalyi showed that people are more likely to grow when they feel included, connected, and valued. When people join forces, they generate a clear sense of collective responsibility and creativity.

Since we were little children, we learned that beauty lies in diversity. However, sometimes as we grow up, we forget this basic principle. It is up to all of us, especially us leaders, to advocate for diversity and inclusion. If we were all the same, things would get boring quickly. Our differences help us to see problems from different angles and to develop unique solutions. The philosopher Heraclitus of Ephesus already stated that "what unites the people is from different proportions". We may have much more things in common than we imagine. We just need to look beyond the visible. Henry Ford argued that "If we were all the same, all think the same way, and all act the same way, there would be no innovation, no problem-solving, no sustained competitive advantage".

4.3 Recognizing and Celebrating Achievements

You must provide team settings where students get the opportunity to discuss projects with the entire group at regular intervals. You must make efforts to celebrate successful milestones reached or critical decisions taken. Populating this lab culture and valuing individual contributions will ensure that the lab as a whole is successful. However, focusing on the overall goal with every member acknowledging the impact of everyone is also important. This balance is crucial in cultivating a healthy and productive lab environment.

In the context of leading a research team, faculty members must recognize that their team members are independent investigators, and there will be situations in which members work on a project without a direct impact on the overall goal of the lab. Yet, the lab members need to be celebrated and recognized at different stages of projects.

This year, focus on recognizing those who have succeeded where others failed, improved since the last time their achievements were recognized, or made a meaningful change or contribution to a product, service, or process. Also, celebrate those who have improved their processes or responded satisfactorily to changing demands, creating an impact on these processes.

Your team members, students, or mentees have made remarkable achievements. The work put in by the team has culminated in a unique and groundbreaking project. The results are out, and your mentee has come out with flying colors at the university. In short, the time to celebrate and recognize the hard work and achievements has arrived.

Milton Keynes UK
Ingram Content Group UK Ltd.
UKHW030908271124
451618UK00011B/329